First Facts®

Spiders

Black Widow Spiders

by Molly Kolpin

Consultant:
Pedro Barbosa, PhD
Department of Entomology
University of Maryland, College Park

CAPSTONE PRESS
a capstone imprint

First Facts is published by Capstone Press,
151 Good Counsel Drive, P.O. Box 669, Mankato, Minnesota 56002.
www.capstonepub.com

 Books published by Capstone Press are manufactured with paper
containing at least 10 percent post-consumer waste.

Library of Congress Cataloging-in-Publication Data
Kolpin, Molly.
 Black widow spiders / by Molly Kolpin.
    p. cm.—(First facts. Spiders)
 Includes bibliographical references and index.
 Summary: "A brief introduction to black widow spiders, including their habitat, food,
and life cycle"—Provided by publisher.
 ISBN 978-1-4296-4519-5 (library binding)
 1. Black widow spider—Juvenile literature. I. Title. II. Series.
QL458.42.T54K65 2011
595.4'4—dc22
                                        2010002255

Editorial Credits
Lori Shores, editor; Veronica Correia, designer; Eric Manske, production specialist

Photo Credits
Alamy/B. Mete Uz, 1; Scott Camazine, 12
Getty Images Inc./Stone/GK Hart/Vikki Hart, cover
iStockphoto/David Orr, 5; Mark Kostich, 8, 17
Newscom, 19; ZUMA Press/NHPA, 20
Photo Researchers Inc/James H. Robinson, 7
Photoshot/Bruce Coleman/Edward L. Snow, 15; George Dodge, 21
Shutterstock/Paula Cobleigh, 11

Essential content terms are **bold** and are defined at the bottom of the page
where they first appear.

Table of Contents

A Warning Sign

A black widow's red mark warns animals of the spider's deadly **venom**. Black widows have the strongest venom of all spiders in North America. Their venom is 15 times stronger than rattlesnake venom. But black widows use only a little venom when they bite.

venom—a harmful liquid produced by some animals

Spider Fact!

No one in the United States has died from a black widow bite in more than 10 years.

female black widow

5

Black widow spiders are **arachnids**. They have two main body parts and eight legs. The female's body is shiny and round. She is 1.5 inches (38 millimeters) long with her legs stretched out.

Male black widows have smaller brown bodies and longer legs. Some males have red or yellow bands on their backs.

arachnid—an animal with four pairs of legs and no backbone, wings, or antennae

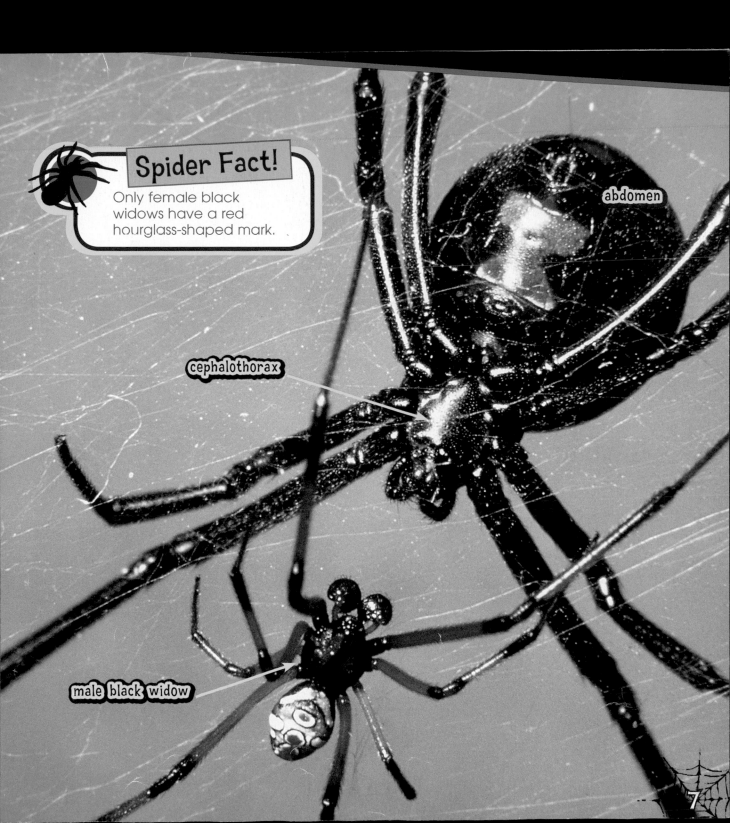

Spider Fact!

Only female black widows have a red hourglass-shaped mark.

abdomen

cephalothorax

male black widow

spinnerets

silk

Hanging Around

Black widow spiders usually live alone. They hang upside down from sticky webs made of **silk**. Spiders use their back legs to pull silk from their **spinnerets**.

Spider Fact!

Some spiders have neat webs. But a black widow's web looks like a tangled mess!

Black Widow World

Black widows live in warm places all over the world. In the United States, most black widow spiders live in the South.

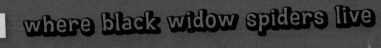

where black widow spiders live

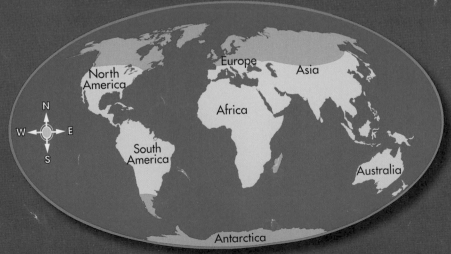

Black widows build webs in dark, protected places. They often make webs outdoors in piles of wood. They also build webs in corners of basements or garages.

Spider Fact!

Black widow venom makes people feel dizzy and achy.

Black Widow Bites

Black widows use venom to kill **prey**. When they bite, venom runs through their sharp, hollow **fangs**. The venom quickly kills the prey.

Dinnertime

Bugs get stuck in a black widow's web. The spider wraps a bug in silk before biting it. Then the spider squirts juices into the bug's body to make it mushy. Finally the spider sucks up its soupy meal.

Spider Fact!

Black widows eat grasshoppers, beetles, and caterpillars.

A Wonderful Life

In the spring, male and female black widows join together to produce young. The female lays between 250 and 700 eggs. She wraps them in an **egg sac** and hangs it from her web. In a few weeks, **spiderlings** crawl out of the egg sac.

Spider Fact!

Animals and insects eat spiderlings. Some spiderlings are eaten by their own brothers and sisters!

egg sac—a small pouch made of silk that holds spider eggs
spiderling—a young spider

Life Cycle of a Black Widow

Newborn

Spiderlings take care of themselves right away.

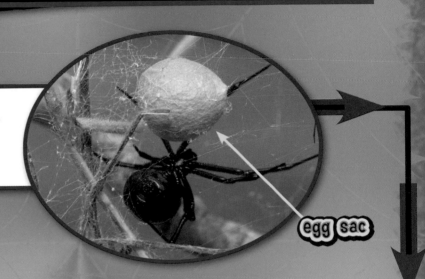

egg sac

Young

As they grow, black widows shed their outer skeleton.

Adult

Black widows are adults after three months.

Growing and Changing

Black widow spiderlings are white or yellow. Each time they **molt**, they become darker. The female's red mark also changes color. At first, the mark is only a white patch. It turns orange after the first few molts. The mark turns red after six to eight molts.

molt—to shed an outer skeleton or layer of skin

spiderlings

Spider Fact!

Female black widows usually live one to three years. Males only live about six months.

What's in a Name?

Black widows earned their names for a good reason. Female black widows sometimes eat their partners. But this practice isn't as common as people once thought.

Amazing but True!

egg sac with eggs and spiderlings

Black widow spiderlings have strong venom even before they hatch. Warriors of the American Indian Gosiute tribe used to pound arrowheads into black widow eggs. The arrowheads were extra deadly with the spider's venom.

Glossary

arachnid (uh-RACK-nid)—an animal with four pairs of legs and no backbone, wings, or antennae

egg sac (EG SAK)—a small pouch made of silk that holds spider eggs

fang (FANG)—a long, pointed toothlike mouthpart

molt (MOHLT)—to shed an outer skeleton or layer of skin

prey (PRAY)—an animal hunted by another animal for food

silk (SILK)—a string made by spiders

spiderling (SPYE-dur-ling)—a young spider

spinneret (spin-nuh-RET)—a body part used to make silk thread

venom (VEN-uhm)—a harmful liquid produced by some animals

Read More

Bishop, Nic. *Spiders.* New York: Scholastic Nonfiction, 2007.

Hartley, Karen, Chris Macro, and Philip Taylor. *Spider.* Bug Books. Chicago: Heinemann Library, 2008.

Lunis, Natalie. *Deadly Black Widows.* No Backbone! The World of Invertebrates. New York: Bearport Publishing, 2009.

Internet Sites

FactHound offers a safe, fun way to find Internet sites related to this book. All of the sites on FactHound have been researched by our staff.

Here's all you do:

Visit *www.facthound.com*

FactHound will fetch the best sites for you!

Index

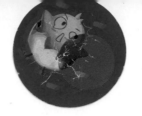